Series edited by Dennis Sharp

YORK

Patrick Nuttgens

Photographs by Keith Gibson

Studio Vista

Produced by November Books Limited, 23–9 Emerald Street, London, WC1N 3QL

Published by Studio Vista Limited, Blue Star House, Highgate Hill, London, N19

Text set by Yendall & Company Limited, Riscatype House, 22–5 Red Lion Court, Fleet Street, London, EC4

Printed by Taylor Garnett Evans and Company Limited, Greycaine Road, Bushey Mill Lane, Watford, Herts.

Bound by Dorstel Press Limited, West Road, Templefields Harlow, Essex

Acknowledgments

The selection of buildings, the critical comments and the inaccuracies are the responsibility of the author. For those facts which are correct he is indebted to members of the York office of the Royal Commission on Historical Monuments, especially Dr Gee and Major Williams, and of the Institute of Advanced Architectural Studies in the University, especially Mr Rymer, Mrs Schubert and Miss Smith.

The maps are based on the Ordnance Survey Map; they are reproduced with the sanction of the Controller of Her Majesty's Stationery Office and with permission from Geographia Ltd.

INTRODUCTION

One thousand nine hundred years ago a Roman legion crossing the River Ouse and needing a camp from which to organise defence and administration in the north of England laid out a fortress on its bank. It was the shape of a playing card, with its narrow edge along the river. The road from the south-west crossed the river, continued through the main gate and became the Via Praetoria, leading to the headquarters of the legion. The street is now known as Stonegate and sitting on the site of the headquarters is the massive and elaborate structure of York Minster.

That was the origin of York. It was an important junction of roads as well as the crossing of a river, and became a centre for the development of the north. The original Roman settlement is still in places visible; and the subsequent history of the city is visible too – a succession of overlays and adaptations as York grew, spreading wider and more raggedly at the edges to become the city of over 100,000 people that it is today.

Eboracum, the place of the yews, occupied about 50 acres and had a population of 5,000. The oldest structures left today came from the occupation – the Multangular Tower that stood at a corner of the perimeter fortifications and a few walls and columns of the principia underneath the Minster.

When the Romans left Britain, York remained a busy trading centre. It received successive waves of occupiers and witnessed the founding of the Christian church in the region. But what mainly survives and gives character to the modern centre of the city is its medieval core.

Devastated after the Norman Conquest, York was rebuilt and expanded. The rectilinear lines of the camp were bent and twisted to suit a new river crossing, new routes to markets and a new urban form dominated by the castle, Clifford's Tower. The derelict walls of the legionary fortress were in part rebuilt and elsewhere built over; and a new defensive wall on the top of a bank above a ditch encircled the city except in one area where a marsh made the wall unnecessary.

Medieval York was 270 acres in area and had eventually a population of about 10,000. It had approximately eight religious houses and 40 parish churches. It was a major centre of commerce and trade and the greatest market in the North. Ships came up the River Ouse, having reached it via the Humber from the North Sea. The staiths, the river banks in the centre of the city, were a harbour, and chains across the river defended it.

The city also became a centre for crafts. Building was continuous for three centuries, leatherwork and stone masonry flourished; but no craft was more distinctive and transcendent than that of stained glass. The Minster and several of the parish churches still reveal the scale and excellence of a craft that made the York school of glass painters famous throughout Europe.

The high water mark of medieval York was the 14th century. Decimated, like many other crowded cities, by the Black Death in 1349, it never fully recovered; and although there was some notable rebuilding in the 15th century, it began to lose its commercial pre-eminence.

There was an interlude of some noise and glory for a hundred years from the middle of the 16th to the middle of the 17th centuries. York became the headquarters of the Council of the North – a body of questionable importance, but considerable panache. That came to an end with the Civil War in 1642–4, when the city's defensive walls were at last put to the test and found to be ineffective. With the restoration of the monarchy in 1660 another chapter of urban life began.

York became a fashionable centre for a reorganised region of huge agricultural estates. New mansions were built in the country, and in the city a succession of solid and impressive town houses for the gentry, wedged together by smaller but still impressive houses for the less fashionable. The city burst out of its walls and new Georgian terraces lined the roads outside the bars. Professions, schools and lunatic asylums came into their own. As the West Riding began to attract the most rapacious generators of industry, York ambled along sociably and complacently with a barely tolerant smile for its reckless neighbours.

And that strange withdrawal from the more adventurous affairs of life continued into and through the industrial revolution of the 19th century. Glass-making took a new direction and the sweet industry begun by Terry's exploded into the chocolate industry, dominated eventually by Rowntree's. But heavy industry did not come to York. It was too far from the sea to be a harbour for the new large boats, too flat to have the water power for mills, too far from the coal mines to become a factory.

What it became was due to a remarkable and infamous man who, like the Romans, saw its

5

potential as a centre for communications. George Hudson set out to 'mak all t'railways cum ti York' and nearly succeeded. The population grew from 17,000 in 1801 to 75,000 in 1901. There were areas of cramped industrial housing and of inadequate services. But the worst aspects of 19th-century *laissez-faire* expansion passed it by. A number of philanthropic industrialists initiated provisions for social welfare; the Church still dominated the city especially in the area around the Minster; the Courts still met and the professions flourished.

Nevertheless, the 20th century saw York relatively in decline. It was like most places, hit by the depression in the 20s and 30s. Then, after World War II, it lay quiet for a while and began another phase of development. In it no event was more significant than the founding of its university.

Today York is a test case for the future of an old settlement. Unusually preserved, as much through apathy as deliberate intent, it finds itself with many of the attributes that a modern humane centre would be lucky to have – small scale, warmth and character, a close mixture of uses, convenience for communications, an obvious potential for pedestrian streets and the proper control of cars. That is why York's buildings and streets are not only historically interesting but also worth analysing and discussing. If York can discover a future for its past, it will have provided a lesson of importance to the European scene and added a new dimension to our lives.

Bibliography

Francis Drake, *Eboracum; or, The History and Antiquities of the City of York.* 1736.

W. Hargrove, *History and Description of the Ancient City of York.* Two vols., York, 1818.

C. B. Knight, *A History of the City of York.* York, 1944.

G. Benson, *An account of the City and County of the City of York from the Reformation to the Year 1925.* York, 1925.

A. Raine. *Medieval York.* London, 1955.

I. P. Pressly, *A York Miscellany.* 1938.

J. B. Morrell, *The City of Our Dreams.* 1940.

Royal Commission on Historical Monuments. *An inventory of the historical monuments in the City of York. Vol. 1. Eboracum: Roman York.* 1962.

P. M. Tillott (ed.), *The City of York (Victoria History of the County of York).* 1961.

York and East Yorkshire Architectural Society Year Books, especially 1956–7.

York Institute of Architectural Study. *Studies in Architectural History*, ed. W. A. Singleton. Vol. I, 1954. Vol. II, 1956.

York Civic Trust Annual Reports. 1946 to date.

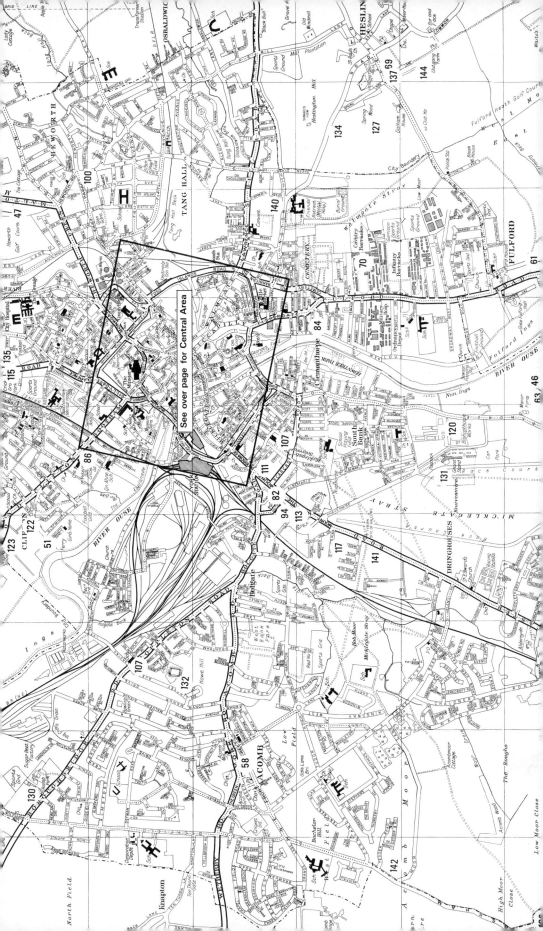

See over page for Central Area

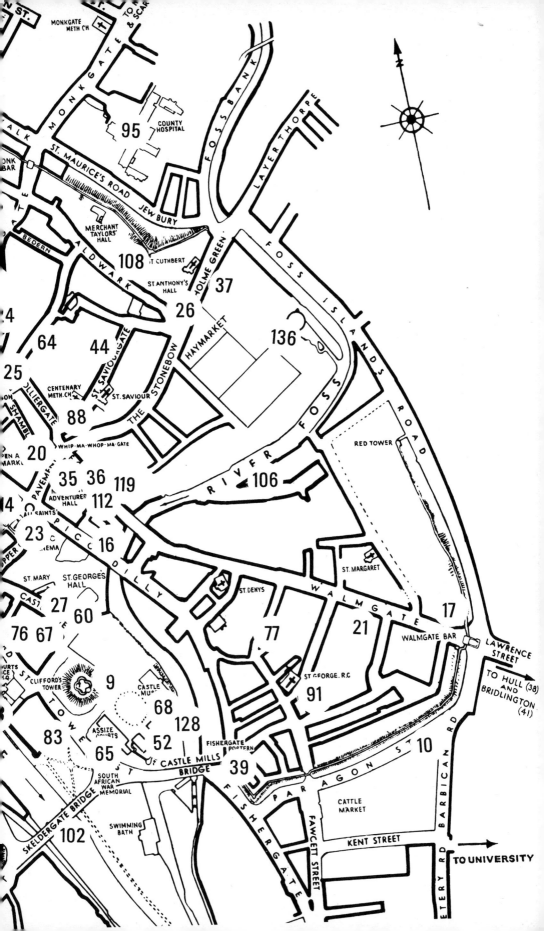

GAZETTEER

1
ROMAN YORK   1st to 4th Centuries

The Romans arrived in York in A.D. 71 and shortly afterwards built the first legionary fortress. Between then and the early 4th century it was rebuilt and altered significantly on at least four occasions. It was a rectangle with rounded corners; its long axis, orientated south-west to north-east, was the line of the present Stonegate (18), and the original river crossing was near the present Guildhall. Its area was 50 acres. There were four gates, one on each side. The aerial photograph of the centre of York shows the remaining parts of the outline of Roman York – the wall forming part of two sides of the rectangle with the Minster in the middle. Across the river grew the Colonia, the civil town, almost from the start. It was a ribbon development and the overall form of it is no longer visible; but remains of houses and other items have been excavated in the area of the settlement.

2
THE MULTANGULAR TOWER
Late 3rd or early 4th Century

The Multangular Tower now forms one of the main features of the Museum Gardens, the park landscaped and planted in the Victorian era around the ruins of the tower and of the abbey (8). It was the west corner tower of the Roman fortifications and is the only one of the angle towers and interval towers left. The original defences had an earthen bank and timber palisades; the stone walls were first built on the banks in the 2nd century; this tower is slightly later. The Roman stonework, with brick throughbands, rises to about 19 ft and there is medieval stonework on top of it for another 11 ft. The inside, similar in construction to the outside, is entered from the grounds of the Public Library (121). With the departure of the Romans from York in the 5th century the walls were altered and breached; the Multangular Tower is the outstanding surviving

2

structure. It may originally have been 60 ft high and contributed to the well-known grandeur of the headquarters of the commander of the army in Britain.

3 ST MARY, BISHOPHILL JUNIOR
11th–13th Centuries

There were until recently two ancient parish churches on Bishophill, to the south of the Ouse, both founded before the Norman Conquest. St Mary Bishophill Senior was demolished a few years ago and parts of it incorporated into a new church (130); Bishophill Junior remains proud of its tower, 11th century on older foundations, which is the oldest specimen of parish church architecture in the city. It has courses of herring-bone masonry and small barbaric windows. The church itself is 12th- and 13th-century, some of it rebuilt and restored in the 19th century.

4 NORMAN HOUSE
Stonegate   12th Century
Architect for adaptation: George G. Pace

The Norman house is an example of contemporary townscape. It straddles, or would have done, the paved way to a hall, and forms a court off the upper end of Stonegate. Its restoration has made an outside square of what was once the inside of a house. After William the Conqueror's devastation of the city its population declined; but it picked up again in the 12th century. Most of the new houses were of wood. This one was at the time an exception, being built of stone and of substantial dimensions.

5 HOLY TRINITY, MICKLEGATE
12th–15th Centuries
Architect for restoration: W. Singleton

Holy Trinity Priory was a Benedictine foundation, a daughter house of the abbey of Marmoutier. It had its own precinct and precinct wall just inside Micklegate Bar (12). The priory was dissolved in 1538 and the nave of the priory church became what is now the parish church of Holy Trinity. It is mainly the work of the late 12th century, though the character of the church inside is much affected (and not

much improved) by the chancel of 1886, and the west end which was recast at the beginning of this century. The tower however is cold and impressive in its unsophisticated plainness; it was built from old stones in 1453.

6
ST JOHN, OUSEBRIDGE
12th–15th Centuries

The church of St John the Evangelist was founded in the 12th century. The interior of the tower, which was later surrounded by other walls, reveals windows of that date. The church is mainly of the 14th and 15th centuries. A steeple fell off the tower in the 16th century and the brick-nog bell turret on the top was made in the 17th century. The east wall is of 1851, when the church was shortened so that North Street could be widened, improbable though this must seem to anyone looking at the street today. However, the changes were not over. The church became redundant and was closed in 1939. In 1956, after ingenious restoration, it was reopened as the Institute of Advanced Architectural Studies, later part of the University of York; and when the Institute moved

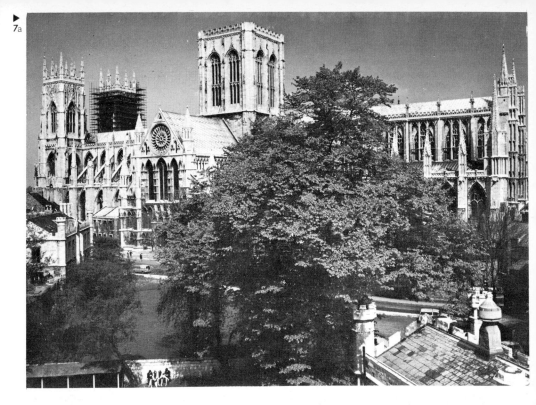

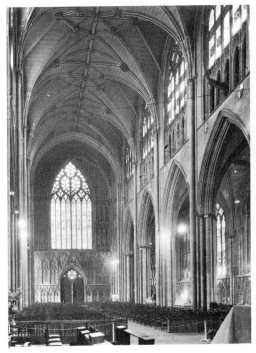

to the King's Manor (38) it became the York Arts Centre. The illustration shows part of it in the latter guise.

7
YORK MINSTER   1227–1472
Architect for restoration: Bernard Feilden

Over 500 ft long and 100 ft wide, with a central tower nearly 200 ft high, York Minster is one of the largest of the English cathedrals and pre-eminent for its mass and volume. It is said that you could put a couple of the smaller cathedrals side by side in the nave and another one on top of them. It sits diagonally on top of the remains of the Roman legionary fortress, facing with liturgical correctness east to west rather than following the geometry of the city; and that was the right place for a Christian church if it was to take over the dominance of the pagan world. It was a missionary outpost run by a group of

clergy – a *monasterium* – hence the name *minster*. But there was never a monastery in the usual sense of the word.

The present building is the fourth on the site. Roughly speaking, the transepts are 13th-century, the nave and choir 14th-century, and the towers are 15th-century. There are later additions, notably after a maniac burnt down part of the Minster in the early years of the 19th century and when it was restored in the 1840s, the north transept being provided with one of the earliest cast-iron roofs in the world. The latest, most elaborate restoration is the result of failing foundations, especially those under the central tower and east end. The structural re-organisation, by Bernard Feilden, is ingenious and worth enquiry. But in addition the cleaning and repainting of the interior is transforming a huge but heavy and plain interior into what it should be – an image of the celestial city. In that

context note the geometrically intricate and structurally daring chapter house (14th-century) and the glory of the whole fabric – the stained glass windows. Some of the glass is from the 12th and 13th centuries, acres of it are 14th-century. The great east window is however early 15th-century; and even the famous Five Sisters grisaille window in the north transept looks clumsy compared to this supreme exercise of the most sophisticated professional skill and inexhaustible vision. The Minster has 117 windows and they contain nearly half the total medieval stained glass in Britain.

8
ST MARY'S ABBEY   *c.* **1270**
The abbey was built outside the city walls in its own precinct of about 12 acres. A wall surrounding the precinct was completed in 1266 and the abbot responsible for it, Simon de Warwick, began then to replace the Norman

church founded in 1089. His church, started in 1270, was elaborate and grand. It had an aisled nave and choir, north and south transepts, and was 350 ft long. The guest house lay to the west, the domestic buildings to the south and the abbot's house (38) to the north-east. What remains is mainly part of the nave; for although excavation has revealed many other parts, the abbey ruins became a quarry for such buildings as the County Gaol and repairs to Beverley Minster. Now the nave, with its richly carved arcading and big empty windows, makes a powerful setting for the York Mystery Plays; the sun sets over the ruins more romantically than it did over the Benedictine Abbey at its dissolution in 1539.

9
CLIFFORD'S TOWER   **13th Century**
York Castle
In the years preceding the Norman Conquest

York had become a great trading centre. It resisted William the Conqueror and in 1069, when he moved north and harried the region, the city was almost completely destroyed by fire. Clifford's Tower is the castle that William erected as the centre of a new feudal administration. It is a motte and had a bailey, now the space between the museums. The structure on top of the earthen mound was at first a wooden keep. But in 1190 there occurred a tragic episode when the Jewish population, attempting to escape massacre, sought shelter there and in their terror set fire to the castle and died in the flames. The stone shell-keep that replaced it dates from the 13th century; it is quatrefoil in shape and had a roof which was destroyed by an explosion in the 17th century. Across the river was another motte, the two mottes thus controlling the river; this is now known as Baile Hill and is currently being excavated.

10
THE CITY WALLS 13th Century

The building of Clifford's Tower altered the form of the city so that it spread away from the Roman core towards the south-east. A defensive wall was thrown round it. It had an earthen bank, a wooden palisade and a moat below. Soon after 1250, stone walls began to be built along the top, and they surrounded the city except for an impassable stretch of water (now drained) near the river Foss, known as the King's Fishpond. With the exception of a relatively small portion destroyed in the 19th century their 4,840 yards are still complete today. The creamy magnesian limestone came from Tadcaster. They have been repaired

frequently, most notably after the siege of 1644. Just after 1800 several attempts were made by the Corporation to take them down, but public opinion won and ultimately their continuous paved interior platform became a public footpath, maintained by the Corporation as a public walk. The walls are the most complete city

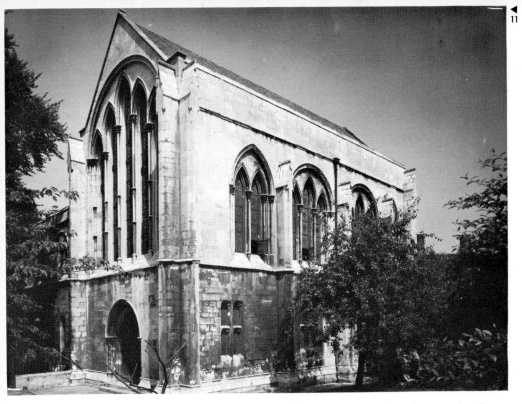

walls in the country and despite constant threats, still serve to keep the nastier aspects of the 20th century outside. Along one side is the cattle market and so it is still possible in the middle of York to hear and smell cattle as well as motor cars. The best short stretch for a quick vigorous walk and excellent views is that from Bootham Bar to Monk Bar, close to the Minster.

11
THE MINSTER LIBRARY 13th Century
The archbishop's palace in the 13th century lay in what is known today as Dean's Park, to the north of the Minster. After the Reformation it fell into disrepair and was later sold and ultimately cleared away. The only surviving part is the chapel, which was repaired in 1813 and became the Minster Library. It is a plain lofty stone building with lancet windows grouped in threes under semicircular arches. Extensions to the building were made later. The library itself is an old and distinguished one.

12
MICKLEGATE BAR 13th–14th Centuries
Micklegate Bar is the main entrance to the medieval city on the road from Leeds, London and the south-west. The word 'bar' means 'gate', the word 'gate' means 'street' in the old dialect. Micklegate, to complete the confusion, was the 'muckle' gate or great street leading in a fine sweep to the Ouse Bridge. The bar, like the other three bars on the main routes, had a barbican, which was removed in the early 19th century. There was also a portcullis and at one time a house built into the upper part of the

bar. The archways flanking the central arch are 18th- to 19th-century and were driven through for easier access by pedestrians and presumably vehicles. Vehicles are to be seen today trying to take advantage of it. Note the little stone figures on the parapet keeping watch over them. Real heads were also hung over the top sometimes.

13
BOOTHAM BAR   **13th–14th Centuries**
Almost on the site of the original Roman gate
to the Via Principalis (Petergate), Bootham Bar
guards the road to the north. Probably the most
attractive of the bars, it is hemmed in by later,
especially 18th-century, buildings; its flight of
steps gives access to the public walk and its
dark forbidding arches to the Minster and the
gentlemen's lavatory. The barbican was removed in 1832 but again public feeling ensured
the saving of the bar itself. The portcullis

inside it was saved similarly 50 years later and
there is every reason to believe that notwith-
standing the most ingenious and extraordinary
traffic proposals the bar is safe – if not the
houses wedged against it which create much of
its charm.

14
ST MARTIN-CUM-GREGORY
Micklegate   **13th–15th Centuries**
The church of St Martin was united with that of

St Gregory in 1586. The latter disappeared; the former survives but in due course has also become redundant. In 1953 its parish was united with that of Holy Trinity further up the hill. Its future is a matter of serious concern because the church is one of the best in York, airy, elegant and spacious, the whitened walls lending even more spirit to the architecture than it had in more Christian times. The nave is basically 13th-century, with a north aisle added in the 14th century and a clerestory added in the 15th century. The overall impression is of the 15th century. There are windows of 14th-century stained glass and some unique pieces by William Peckitt, the 18th-century glass painter who is buried in the church. His widow erected a window, in wonderfully inappropriate style, to his memory. There are other fine furnishings, especially the font, pulpit, bread shelves and alms box, and a brick tower at the west end, of 19th-century vintage.

15
LADY ROW   c. 1320
Goodramgate

The oldest houses in York are in the terrace which forms the boundary of the churchyard of Holy Trinity. They are now a row of shops, with jettied upper floors, and have been much altered throughout their history; but the construction of the houses reveals their date as c. 1320 and makes them some of the oldest small houses in Europe.

16
MERCHANT ADVENTURER'S HALL
1357–68

The York mercers and merchants became
merchant adventurers in the 15th century and
their religious, social and commercial centre
was this extensive 14th-century timbered
building. Its structure reflects their aspiring
name and its survival, despite mixed fortunes
and heavy restoration, testifies to the quality of
their work. The lower hall or undercroft was
the hospital for members who had fallen on
hard times; the weighty wooden pillars in the

middle are unusual. The upper floor has the
great hall, where timber construction can be
studied at its most skilful and evocative. The
house on the north side of the hall is a later
but not unremarkable addition.

17
WALMGATE BAR   14th Century

First mentioned in the 12th century, Walmgate
Bar was built in the 14th century when the
section of the walls in that area was reconstructed. It is the area around the road to Hull
and the one in which most of the unfit 19th-

century housing was to be seen until recent massive clearances and some good rebuilding. This bar is the only one to retain its barbican and thus gives a lively impression of the form of the medieval gates and the hazards that an invader had to face. It was not very effective, however, in 1644, and was greatly damaged and later repaired. On the inside of the bar is a 16th-century house over the archway, built of timber and forming an extension to the accommodation within the stone structure.

18
STONEGATE 14th Century and later

The best set piece of the old city, Stonegate is on the line of the Via Praetoria, whose surface is about 6 ft below the present street surface. What is to be seen today is essentially a

medieval street, with houses dating mainly
from the 14th to the 19th centuries. Some have
been developed in depth at right angles to the
street and there are small tight irregular courts
and alleys opening off the street in several
places, some flanked with good 18th-century
houses. At the upper end Stonegate was
funnelled to become Minster Gates, the paved
entry to the Minster precinct and the steps to
the south door of the Minster. Unfortunately in
1903 a new road, Deangate, was driven across
the precinct beside the Minster and severed
Stonegate from the ruined precinct. There are
enlightened proposals to make Stonegate
pedestrian, and if Deangate is ever closed to
traffic the central area of the city will be
unequalled in Britain.

19
HIGH PETERGATE
14th Century and later
Part of the Via Principalis, High Petergate
became an important medieval street leading
from Bootham Bar to the west door of the
Minster. Its houses have mainly 18th-century
exteriors and there are some good panelled
interiors. Precentor's Court (49) opens off it.

20
SHAMBLES   **14th Century and later**
The best known of the medieval streets of York,
but not as medieval as it looks. The jettied
upper stories almost touch across the road. It
was once the street of butchers, now of tourists
and small specialised shops; the shop fronts
are mostly modern in traditional style, but there
are remains of the earlier butchers' stalls. The
present market opens neatly off it.

21
BOWES MORRELL HOUSE
Walmgate   **Late 14th Century**
Architects for restoration: Brierley, Leckenby
and Keighley
A pleasant timber-framed house of the late 14th
century, it enlivens an otherwise ruined street.
It was restored for the York Civic Trust by the
architects Brierley, Leckenby and Keighley and
opened in 1966, named after the founder of the
Trust. Its plan is said to be unique in the city.
There are 17th-century additions at the rear.

22
ALL SAINTS, NORTH STREET
14th–15th Centuries
Architect for restoration: E. Ridsdale Tate
Unobtrusively set back from the river on its
unfashionable bank and now helplessly overshadowed by a multi-storey hotel, All Saints is
still the expert's place of pilgrimage. For it
contains the best stained glass in York and
some of the best in Europe. Some is 14th-
century, with its hot and sombre yellows, but
the best is the 15th-century group in the north
aisle; the Corporal Works of Mercy seem fun
to carry out, and the Fifteen Last Days of the
World are colourfully symbolic. There are

pieces of early architecture but the dominant
style is 15th-century, including the high narrow
spire. Earlier this century the incumbent, a man
of positive ideas, unstinting charity and High
Church leanings, filled the interior with an
abundant variety of church furniture; now
much simplified, it still gives a rare impression
of what a medieval church must have looked
like. He also added a hermit's cell to the west

wall, with concrete supports that resemble wood and a peep-hole inside that looks down the length of the church to the altar. Unfortunately there is no longer a hermit in the cell.

23
ALL SAINTS, PAVEMENT
14th–15th Centuries

The octagonal lantern lodged ungraciously on top of a square tower is the most distinguished and sophisticated part of All Saints. Much of the church dates from the 14th century, but the clerestory and tower with the lantern were built between 1475 and 1501. Of the post-Reformation period are the pulpit and sounding board. The roads immediately surrounding it have been the cause of a series of amputations. Most of the churchyard was removed in the 17th century, the chancel was removed in the 18th century, and a wing on the south side was removed in the mid-20th century. There is still, however, plenty of the church left.

24
HOLY TRINITY, GOODRAMGATE
14th–15th Centuries

The churchyard, quiet and unpretentious, is entered through a gate that can easily be missed

in Goodramgate, beside the oldest houses in the city (15). The church has a nave and two aisles, in the York manner of giving them all gables and roofs of equal height. The nave is essentially 14th-century, but the church as a whole is a 15th-century piece, with stained glass in the east window of 1472. What creates its unique and cosy character is the equipment of the 18th century – the altar piece, the two-decker pulpit and the battery of box-pews with little doors and quiet corners for eating peppermints during the sermon. Their silhouette follows the irregularity of the floor, which seems to have sunk in every direction. The levels are unusual. Steps go down when you would expect them to go up. Not surprisingly, the church is much loved and is being cared for, although redundant.

25
KING'S SQUARE   14th–18th Centuries
Made from a disused churchyard, the square at the top of the Shambles reveals more vividly than the Shambles themselves the character of York, with closely juxtaposed buildings of different periods grouped tightly around small urban spaces. Houses and old workshops, now used as shops and offices, date from the 14th to the 18th centuries, with a modern intrusion in no particular style.

26
ST ANTHONY'S HALL   1453
Peaseholme Green
Architect for restoration: W. Singleton
The guild of St Anthony was incorporated in 1446, and built a hall and chapel on the corner of Aldwark and Peaseholme Green. A brick and timber building, it has a fine hall, formerly aisled, on the first floor. There are additions later than the 15th century, especially the many fireplaces. It has had several uses – as a workhouse, a house of correction, a knitting school and a military hospital in the Civil War; but in 1953, having been thoroughly restored by the York Civic Trust, it became the Borthwick Institute of Historical Research, now part of the University of York.

ST MARY, CASTLEGATE   15th Century
Architect for restoration: Herbert Butterfield
An inscription found during restoration of the church suggests that there was a very early, pre-Conquest church on the site; the present stylish and dignified edifice dates from the 15th century, though there are portions of 12th- and 13th-century work. The tower with its octagonal spire is the tallest in York and is a landmark. For that reason among others it is often suggested that the church would make an admirable tourist, guide and information centre. It is unused and redundant, which is a pity because it was completely restored by Butterfield in 1870 and it has unusually good seating.

ST WILLIAM'S COLLEGE   15th Century
College Street
Huddling below the east end of the Minster and linked on all sides to other buildings and courts, St William's College is exactly the right scale to look at and one of the most entrancing and informal buildings to visit. It was built as a college for chantry priests of the Minster between 1465 and 1467. Their behaviour lent some colour to the precinct, it is said, but in any case the college was sold to private owners after the Reformation. The courtyard porch and the main stair were added in the 17th century. After being used for some years as flats, it was bought by the Convocation of York in 1906 for a meeting place, and restored. The great halls above are roofed impressively in timber.

ST OLAVE   15th and 18th Centuries
Marygate
The church is on the edge of the precinct of St Mary's Abbey, and its graveyard uses some of the abbey grounds. It signposts the gateway and looks thoroughly medieval, which is a tribute to its designers, for the 15th-century church was badly damaged while being used as a platform for guns in the Civil War and was largely rebuilt (in the right style) in 1721. The chancel, of 1879, is by George Fowler Jones.

GUILDHALL and COUNCIL OFFICES
15th, 19th and 20th Centuries
Architect for Council Offices: E. G. Mawbey
Meetings of the Town Council originally took place in a council chamber on Ouse Bridge, which it shared with so many other buildings that in 1564 the bridge fell down. Meantime the Guildhall, or common hall, was built beside the Ouse, almost across the place of the original Roman crossing. It was a joint venture of the City and the Guild of St Christopher and was built between 1446 and 1459. Its unique feature is the double row of massive oak pillars, rising the full height of the hall and supporting the roof. In 1942 it was gutted during an air raid and rebuilt between 1956 and 1960 as a replica of the original (except for some glass and the light fittings). The admirable offices and council chamber adjoining it along the river bank were an addition of 1889 by E. G. Mawbey, the city surveyor.

ST MARTIN-LE-GRAND
Coney Street   **15th and 20th Centuries**
Architect for restoration: George G. Pace
An air raid in 1942 almost wholly destroyed the spacious and impressive parish church in the middle of the busiest shopping street in the city. It was built between 1437 and 1449. Out of the fragments that remained an imaginative complex has been created by the architect for its restoration. The south aisle has been rebuilt as a Shrine of Remembrance to citizens who died in World War II, and a paved court defined by modern stonework has been made beside it. The huge clock fixed to the east end, which at this

◀
30

point punctuates the street and gives some emphasis to its dreary modern buildings, dates from 1668; the brackets are later.

ALL SAINTS COTTAGE and
31 NORTH STREET   Late 15th Century
On the corner of North Street and the paved passage to All Saints, the half-timbering with its bracing makes this an example of the Wealden house; its detail, such as the carving on the corner post, indicates its former importance. The old shop on the corner was until

recently a rare slice of the life of the old, small scale, crowded, rattling city.

33
85–9 MICKLEGATE   Late 15th Century
Most of the houses in Micklegate were rebuilt in the 18th century. This 3-storey group remains indicative of the character of the medieval street, in front of Holy Trinity churchyard. It does not appear on Speed's map of 1610 but it must have been there, or at least something like it – for it was recently drastically restored and the rendering on the front removed to expose the timber framing – an aesthetic mistake even if archaeologically defensible.

34
ST MICHAEL-LE-BELFREY   1525–36
The medieval church on the site, close to the Minster, was the parish church for people who lived in Minster Yard. The present church was completed just in time for the Reformation. It thus fills a niche in the history of York architecture. Guy Fawkes was baptised here in 1570. The west front was drastically restored in 1867; the restrained paving in front of it is an enlightened memorial to Dean Milner White, a founder of the York Civic Trust; it was laid in 1966.

35
THE HERBERT HOUSE   1557
Pavement
An outstanding example of Tudor domestic architecture, the house was built by a wealthy

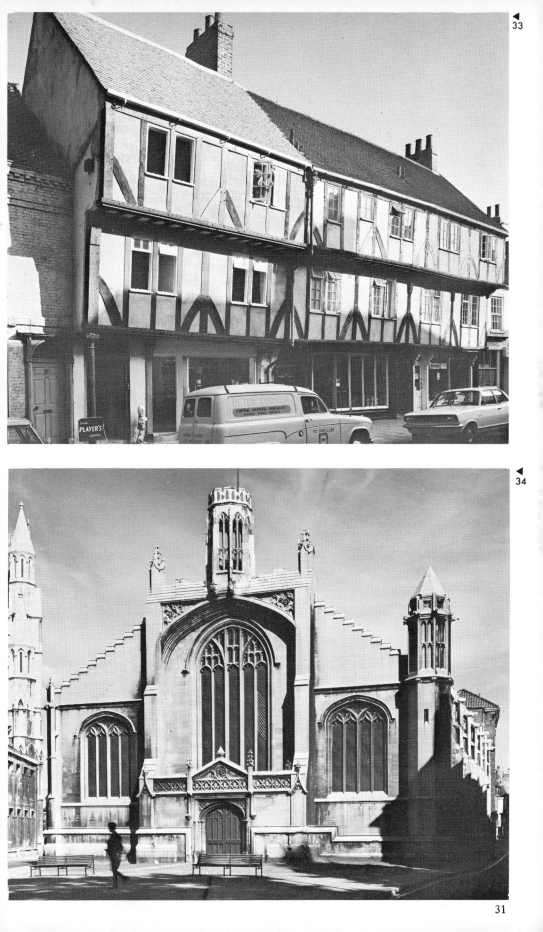

a few years later in half-timbering, joined to-gether by a link block of 1648 which has since been altered. There is a hall on the first floor. The mixture of styles and details and the closing of the yard by a cross wing over an opening make this an attractive space; but disillusion follows swiftly once you get to the end.

37
THE BLACK SWAN   *c.* 1560
Peaseholme Green

The oldest building in York used as a public house. There are probably the remains of an early 15th-century house beneath it, but most of the present house was built in about 1560 by Sir Martin Bowes, who was Lord Mayor of London before coming back to York. Other features date from 1670. The interior is famous, not just for drinking, but for some remarkable woodwork and painted panels on the first floor.

38
THE KING'S MANOR

13th–20th Centuries
especially 1560–1640
Architects for restoration: Feilden and Mawson

It started as the abbot's house of St Mary's Abbey (8), with heavy stone walls of the 13th-century, the lower courses of which survive. A major rebuilding took place in the 15th century, when Abbot Sever commissioned much of the brickwork that characterises the entrance front and the first quadrangle. The King's Manor received its new name and a new function after the Reformation and the failure of the Pilgrim-

Elizabethan family, the Herberts. The ground floor has been altered but the upper floors of this 3-storey house, the two upper floors of which are jettied, reveal inside, as well as out, the scale and substance of the family. The barge boards are decorated with contrasting motifs. The entry to the right leads directly into Lady Peckitt's Yard.

36
LADY PECKITT'S YARD   *c.* 1560
The back of the Herbert House forms a yard with another house, also built by the Herberts

age of Grace in 1536. It became the head-quarters of the Council of the North, which lasted about a hundred years until the Civil War. The best parts, for example the quadrangle and the state rooms, were recastings of around 1600. Its later fortunes were mixed; it became a girls' school, an elementary school and at one time flats for town councillors. In 1833 a School of the Blind was founded in memory of William Wilberforce, and gradually took over the whole of the Manor; the Headmaster's House in the forecourt was designed by Walter Brierley in 1900 and is a brilliant piece of pastiche which deceives many an architectural historian. In 1963 the Corporation, having acquired the Manor, leased it to the newly-founded University of York, and its bold straightforward restoration and the completion of the complex with new buildings by Feilden and Mawson have reconstituted it as one of the most

33

fascinating as well as historically baffling pieces of architecture in the north of England.

39
FISHERGATE POSTERN   16th Century
Fishergate Postern with its tower is one of the later features of the city wall. The river Foss had begun to silt up and the tower and postern were ordered to be built by the Corporation in 1502. The roof is 18th-century. The tower strongly marks the termination of the wall across the river from the castle; the castle itself controlled the intervening area where the Foss and the Ouse join; a chain across the river Ouse added another link to the defences; and then the wall started up again at the Baile Hill.

40
JACOB'S WELL   **16th Century**
Trinity Lane
A strange and puzzling building to which much has happened; it is said to be the late medieval house to which the last prioress of St Clement's Nunnery retired when it was dissolved in 1536. But much of it is later. It became a public house in the 19th century, but was rescued and made respectable in the early 20th century as a

church hall. Its richly carved doorway provides a nice emphasis in the lane.

41
OUSE BRIDGE INN   **16th Century–1898**
King's Staith
The datestone over the door announces the public house as of 1898. But the house seems much earlier and must be the last of the old

houses on the Staith at the end of the Water Lanes that led from Castlegate to the river. It was well situated close to Ouse Bridge and to the 'common jakes' at the end of the bridge. The rising of the Ouse regularly floods the public house, as well as others further down the river, where boats are kept to enable determined customers to escape at the last minute; this one records on the wall in the bar the various levels that the river has reached. It gets quite close to

the ceiling when presumably only the heads of the customers can be seen.

42

THE TREASURER'S HOUSE   *c.* **1600**

Facing the Minster and its chapter house, the Treasurer's House is on the site of the medieval one occupied by the treasurer to the minster. That is why it has long had its name. It was, however, built after the abolition of the

treasurership and is essentially a private house, originally larger than it is now (see Gray's Court, 48). Its plan is of the 'H' type, and its date about 1600. The ogee gables are probably a little later. It has good 18th-century interiors and a formidable staircase: also a hall rising through two floors which is largely the result of restoration by Mr Frank Green, who bought the house shortly before 1900, reassembled and unified it, filled it with valuable furniture and presented it to the National Trust in 1930.

43
INGRAM HOUSE   c. 1640
90 Bootham

One of several groups of almshouses in York, Ingram House was built as Sir Arthur Ingram's Hospital shortly before 1640. It was designed to have a central tower over a chapel and sets of rooms for 10 poor widows. The general plan survives, the sets of rooms having been converted by the trust that owns it into four flats. The Norman doorway with chevron ornament in the central tower is thought to have been acquired from Holy Trinity Priory at its dissolution, and brought here later.

44
ST SAVIOURGATE UNITARIAN   1693
CHAPEL

The plan is cruciform, the area of the four wings being roughly the same as the area of the

crossing. It is a very plain brick building of 1693, with later windows. Its centralised plan and austere character make it the most distinctively nonconformist chapel in the city, wholly uncompromising and making no concessions to anyone.

45
CUMBERLAND HOUSE   c. 1695
King's Staith

It was built for Alderman William Cornwell at the beginning of the 18th century, has changed hands many times and was until recently a YWCA club. Beautifully sited on the riverside, the King's Staith, it is entered from Cumberland Street. The rising river covers the stone plinth and floods the cellars but, if fortune smiles, just leaves the front door clear. Rather Dutch in its proportions, it has handsome stone quoins and centre piece and an excellent cornice.

46
MIDDLETHORPE HALL   1699–1701
Bishopthorpe

The hall was built for Thomas Barlow, master cutler of Sheffield. Its front reveals similarities with Cumberland House (45); together with that house it provoked comment as introducing the new architectural fashions to York. The side wings are of the middle of the 18th century.

47
CASTLE HOWARD   1699–1759
Architects: Sir John Vanbrugh and Nicholas Hawksmoor

Although this book does not generally include buildings outside York or its immediate surroundings, it cannot omit Castle Howard in the North Riding, which initiated the country house building boom that transformed the Yorkshire landscape in the 18th century, and left it almost littered with country houses. It is also supreme among them. It was the playwright Sir John Vanbrugh's first architectural design; its layout and internal planning broke new ground and established English Baroque. Hawksmoor (who was a professional architect) collaborated with him. The hall and most of the first part of the house is Vanbrugh's; so is the Temple of the Four Winds; but the Mausoleum is wholly Hawksmoor's. Castle Howard, as Walpole observed, is not just a house; with its landscape and grounds it almost forms a city.

48
GRAY'S COURT   **17th and 18th Centuries**
Gray's Court is the other half of the Treasurer's House (42). It opens off the stony College

Street, and with its trees and cobbles and elusive air of battered elegance makes one of the most soothing urban spaces in the city. The division of the house occurred in the early 18th century; this was the northern wing and it was renamed by its owner at the end of that century.

49
PRECENTOR'S LANE and COURT
Early 18th Century
The precinct at the west end of the Minster became for a time heavily over-built. With the creation of Duncombe Place it was cleared up,

by Duncombe Place. The houses on it are of the early 18th century, with casements characteristic of that date and a large proportion of glass to wall. The doorways are mostly insertions of the early 19th century, although that of No. 23 on the extreme right is of 1780. The houses sit on older ones, for among them is one (No. 25) described as the birthplace of Guy Fawkes, who was baptised in St Michael-le-Belfrey on the other side of the street in 1570.

51
WATER END and ELLISON'S TERRACE
Clifton Green   **Early 18th and early 19th Centuries**

Clifton, like Acomb (see 58), was a village outside York, lying on the old Roman route to the north. With the Georgian extension it gradually met the city, and Clifton Green became the centre of a residential suburb that was developed around the triangle of grass during the next 100 years. Ellison's Terrace was completed by 1819; the cottages joined to it are older; the Green itself is still the site of fairs.

52
THE DEBTORS' PRISON   1701–5
York Castle
Architect: William Wakefield

The centre-piece of the 18th-century buildings that enclose the castle precinct, the Debtors' Prison was built with stone from the ruined St Mary's Abbey, and reckoned in its time to be the finest gaol in Europe. The gaoler lived here and, originally, prisoners of all kinds. The building, with its projecting double wings,

but fortunately not so as to destroy the early 18th-century buildings that make Precentor's Court. Entered by the narrow Precentor's Lane from the Minster or through an alley from High Petergate, Precentor's Court is a simple and very private small urban space in the heart of the city.

50
23–7 HIGH PETERGATE
     Early 18th Century

The Via Principalis of the legionary fortress, this section of the old High Petergate lost some of its character when the street was cut in half

attached giant pilasters and especially the rusticated ones on each side of the door, was thought to be by Vanbrugh, who was building Castle Howard in similar vein at the time. It was probably by William Wakefield, who worked with him. It is now part of the museum, and the old prisoners' yard at the side contains a reconstituted Edwardian street.

53
THE RED HOUSE 1714
Duncombe Place

It was built by Sir William Robinson in what was Lop Lane, a narrow street leading to the west gate of the Minster precinct. Duncombe Place was created in 1860 by the demolition of some houses on the south side of Petergate. Robinson's house thus became more exposed; the cutting of St Leonard's Crescent had already put it on a corner; its red colour wash gives it prominence and distinction. The

stones on the side are from the ruined St Leonard's Hospital; the alternating proud and recessed planes of the front are remarkable.

54
JUDGES' LODGING   *c.* 1720
Lendal
This original house, stylistically much in advance of its time, was built by a physician of the County Hospital. The stone centre panel has

bold and skilful carvings. The lodgings of the judges were then in Coney Street, but in 1806 the house was acquired and became the residence for the peripatetic judges on their circuit.

55
THE MANSION HOUSE   1726
Often said to be by Lord Burlington, who was designing the Assembly Rooms, it was in fact

in a quite different style, resembling that of Roger Morris. The idea of having a Lord Mayor's residence for his year of office put York ahead of London, which produced the equivalent a few years later. The ground floor front that lurks behind the flowers is mainly plaster work on brick. The state room and banqueting hall spans the front of the first floor. This house has beautiful panelling, with crisp detail, and is impeccably kept.

56
ASSEMBLY ROOMS   1731–2
Architect: Lord Burlington

A seminal building in the history of architecture. Its author was Lord Burlington, the fastidious patron of the age of elegance, who brought back from the Grand Tour the ideas of Palladio, and imposed his taste on fashionable early 18th-century England. The Assembly Rooms were for weekly assemblies, concerts and race-week balls, but were never very successful except as architecture. They are a version of Palladio's Egyptian Hall in Roman Corinthian (or one end is) and a skilful piece of cosmetic work. The upper storey is made of timber and the marbled columns are superbly painted to deceive you. Restoration was carried out by the corporation in 1951 and the Rooms are probably more attractive than they were under Burlington's intolerant eye. A new entrance front was designed by J. P. Pritchett in 1828.

57
WANDESFORD HOUSE   1739
Bootham

This was Mary Wandesford's Hospital and her bust can be seen on a pedestal on the outsize pediment over the three central bays. It was also known as the Old Maids' Hospital and housed 10 poor gentlewomen over the age of 50. It is plain but pleasant, and an otherwise dull façade is articulated by the brick arches.

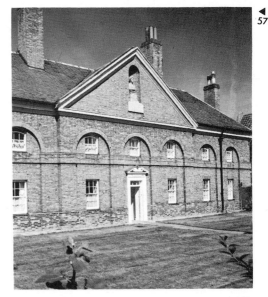

58
ACOMB HOUSE *c.* **1750**
Front Street, Acomb
Architects for restoration: Weightman and Bullen
Acomb was a village separate from York, but now forms one of its main growth areas. Front Street is surrounded by acres of mediocre housing but the street itself survives and Acomb House has been restored by the architects Weightman and Bullen as their own office, and a house. Built in the first half of the 18th century, it has rococo decoration in the splendid first floor drawing room, which must be later. Well restored to an appropriate new use.

◀◀
60

59
MICKLEGATE HOUSE *c.* **1752**
This was the town house of the Bourchiers of Beningbrough. With its wide front, stone bands and simple fenestration, it suggests the work of John Carr but there is no evidence that he designed it. Having later become a warehouse for a chemical firm it was acquired in the 1960s by the University of York and restored as a research centre. Many of the rooms have lost their original fittings but there are still some good interiors and panelling, and a stylish staircase with the characteristic York motif of three different types of baluster marching upwards in sequence.

60
FAIRFAX HOUSE **1755–62**
Castlegate
Architect: John Carr
Sadly decayed and arrogantly painted inside in a wholly tasteless manner, this house is one of the more pathetic survivals in York. It was built for the 9th Viscount Fairfax and cost in its time an enormous sum of money. The bands of stone marking the floors on the front are typical of Carr, the window margins and

lintols on the first floor more refined than his usual.

61
NABURN LOCK and BANQUETING
HOUSE
1757, 1823

The river Ouse, often silting up, has always been troublesome for navigation. Naburn, a few miles downstream, was given a weir in 1741. The lock and dam were opened in 1757 and in the early 19th century a steam packet plied between York and Hull. Even so, the building of the banqueting house in 1823 (in

the background) for use by the trustees seemed extravagant, however inelegant its architecture.

62
BAR CONVENT
c. **1760**
Blossom Street
Architect: Thomas Atkinson

The Bar Convent is on the corner of Blossom Street and Nunnery Lane just outside Mickle-gate Bar. Hence its name. It was opened in 1686, long before Catholics were allowed freedom of worship elsewhere, for the education of

Catholic girls. The handsome but undisting-
uished Georgian façade is of the 1760s. Hidden
away in the heart of the building and undetect-
able from the outside is the chapel, a delicious
piece of Baroque with a domed oval sanctuary.

63
BISHOPTHORPE PALACE 1763–9
Bishopthorpe
Architect for façade: Thomas Atkinson
The home of the Archbishops of York. The
river front contains the oldest parts, though the
13th-century façade on that side was largely
rebuilt in the 17th century. But what you see
from the road is the front by Thomas Atkinson
of 1763–9, one of the earliest and most imaginative exercises of 18th-century whimsy,
disguising what would otherwise be a plain
7-bay 2-storey house. The gatehouse with its
crockets and pinnacles is of the same date. The
whole environment, of house, offices, out-
buildings and landscape, is a delightful set
piece.

64
20 ST ANDREWGATE c. 1770–80

It was the house of Thomas Atkinson the

rchitect, who died in 1798. Presumably he
esigned his own house. It has a huge pediment
nd central features elaborated to emphasise a
ymmetry which would otherwise be invisible
1 a narrow street. The street is almost wholly
uined, partly by a consistent lack of decision
n the part of the authorities, and No. 20,
owever well proportioned itself, gives little
lea of its former dominance.

5
SSIZE COURTS 1773–7
rchitect: John Carr
eripatetic courts met in the castle frequently

during the Middle Ages. After the building of
the new gaol, John Carr of York designed the
Assize Court building, which was strengthened
and restored in the 1960s. It has a handsome
cornice and balustrade, punctuated with rather
lonely urns and a lion and unicorn.

66
BOOTHAM PARK HOSPITAL 1777
Architect: John Carr
The York Lunatic Asylum was established in
1772, and was in the forefront of hospital
development; there were only four asylums in
the country at the time. Although there have

been later additions, the simple dignity of John Carr's design survives – a testimony to his capacity to design cheaply in the fashionable manner. Mismanagement of the asylum led to changes in the early 19th century; meantime the Friends' Retreat had been founded to do what Bootham Park had not by then achieved.

67
CASTLEGATE HOUSE *c.* 1780
Castlegate
Architect: John Carr
Castlegate House was built for the Recorder of the City. The decorative features of the front include large brick arches forming a superficial arcade along the first floor, and neat balusters under the windows.

68
THE CASTLE MUSEUM 1780
York Castle
Architect: John Carr
This building became the Female Prison after being built to increase the general accommodation in the gaol. It is almost the mirror image of the architect's Assize Courts (65) on the other side of the green. In 1932 all the

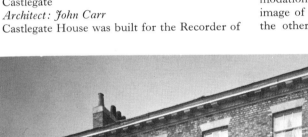

PRIVATE
NO
PARKING

◄◄
69

prisons were wound up and the buildings sold to the Corporation, even though the precinct was not officially in the City of York. It was later used to house Dr Kirk's collection of bygones, and has been transformed into the famous Castle Museum, with comprehensive and unique collections of everyday pieces, and streets of mainly genuine houses with Georgian and Victorian shops displaying wholly genuine merchandise.

69
MORE HOUSE   *c.* 1780
Heslington
Architects for restoration: Tom Adams Design
Associates

Formerly the vicarage for the parish church of Heslington, it became redundant upon the building of a smaller vicarage on adjacent ground. The arrival of the university across the road in 1963 gave it a new use; it was restored for the Catholic Chaplaincy (staffed by Ample-forth Abbey) by Tom Adams. The boldly projecting bay windows rising two storeys, the door details and the cornice give it a family resemblance to Fulford House nearby.

70
CAVALRY BARRACKS　　　　1795
Fulford

The cavalry barracks, of which the illustration shows part of the Officers' Mess, were the first part of a major development that continued for over 100 years after the reforms initiated by William Pitt in 1792. The coat of arms is made of Coade Stone, the astonishingly imperishable artificial stone invented by Coade in the latter half of the 18th century. The secret of its composition died with his widow. The date-stone says 'Coade London 1796'.

71
BOOTHAM SCHOOL　　　　1797–1803
Bootham
Architect: Peter Atkinson

The school was founded in 1822 and moved into its present buildings, or the nucleus of them, in 1846. The many additions and alterations since then have not harmed the decorous and unassuming Georgian front of Bootham or its interior, which is well preserved. Peter Atkinson, the designer of the house, was the partner of John Carr of York (see 133, the Assembly Hall).

1 and 2 MINSTER COURT   18th Century
There is nothing historically remarkable about
these houses, which are informally grouped on
three sides of an open court close to the Minster
and adjoining the Treasurer's House (42).
Their plans are confused; the house on the right
is a late 18th-century covering for a medieval
house behind it. Together they suggest how
pleasantly arcadian the Minster precinct must
have been before a road was driven through it
along the south of the Minster in 1903.

73
21 HIGH PETERGATE   18th Century
Just a pleasant fragment of York streetscape.
The narrow doorway with its arched head and
the frieze across the building with standard
18th-century ornament might be found echoed
elsewhere; but the large bow window on the
first floor so erratically but rightly placed gives a
typically York informality to the façade.

74
54 MICKLEGATE   18th Century
This was first a private house and latterly a
convent school. The doorway is selected to
illustrate the quality of the Georgian doorways
in York.

75
OUSE BRIDGE   1810–20
Architect: Peter Atkinson

Constructed slowly and with interruptions, the stone bridge with its heavily champfered voussoirs, was the last in a series of bridges constructed since the 12th century at the main crossing of the Ouse. The earlier Roman crossing was further upstream. This one had first a timber bridge and later a stone bridge, which, at about the time of a disastrous collapse in 1564 had a chapel, a council chamber, a tollbooth and nearly 20 shops on it.

76
FRIENDS' MEETING HOUSE
Clifford Street   **1816 and later**
Architects: Watson and Pritchett

One of the principal religious bodies in York,

the Quakers rebuilt the meeting houses in 1816 to provide accommodation for 1,200 persons. Clifford Street, from which they are entered, was constructed in 1884 and the entrance changed; but the main meeting house, while surrounded by new buildings, remained.

77
GEORGE STREET   **1818, 1844**
Off Walmgate

George Street, described by Hargrove as a 'row of new dwellings' in 1818 was created as a link between part of Walmgate and the cattle market outside the walls. It was widened and new houses were built in 1844 which probably include those illustrated – small but well-designed working-class housing that was not bettered by later examples.

78
YORK SAVINGS BANK   **1819**
St Helen's Square
Architect: J. P. Pritchett

The York Savings Bank was founded in 1816 and the building was commissioned from the leading Yorkshire architect of his time. It is influenced by Soane's Bank of England and by continental detail, but unusually for York is constructed of a stone that catches all the dirt that will not settle on the other buildings.

79
THEATRE ROYAL   **1821, 1866–88, 1967**
St Leonard's Place
Architect for modernisation: Patrick Gwynne

The theatre fronts on St Leonard's Place, which was created as a new street in 1834. Before that time it was entered from Lop Lane, now Duncombe Place, where the stage door is. A remodelling in the 1820s followed by new upper circles and many other major alterations by John Coleman from 1866 to 1888 made the interior as satisfying, cheerful and decorative as a theatregoer could wish. The ecclesiastical-looking façade was constructed at the end of the century.

In 1967 brilliant reconstruction made it unexpectedly the best piece of modern architecture in York. The stage was modernised, the auditorium refurbished; and beside it the architect, Patrick Gwynne, used something of the design concept he had devised for a restaurant on the Serpentine in Hyde Park, and created, with the help of the engineer R. A. Sefton Jenkins, a new version of pointed arches and vaults in modern reinforced concrete impeccably specified and constructed. That left the perimeter free to be a transparent envelope of glass through which people look strangely attractive as they eat and drink; from the inside passers by look moderately attractive too. The side of the old theatre forms a stone wall inside the foyer and the snaking stairway sucks you

into the green interior of the auditorium. A new exterior arcade at the floor of the theatre is good for display as well as walking; only the signs above the entrance lack the sophistication and wit of the whole concept.

80

YORKSHIRE MUSEUM and the 1827–30 TEMPEST ANDERSON HALL and 1912
Architects: William Wilkins (1823) and
E. Ridsdale Tate (1912)

The Yorkshire Philosophical Society was founded in 1823 and employed as the architect of its museum William Wilkins, best known for his works at Cambridge (Downing and the entrance screen at Kings) and at London (University College and the National Gallery). The museum is in his most scholarly Greek Revival style, and houses among other things invaluable remains of medieval stonework displayed in the most delightfully casual manner.

The Tempest Anderson Hall was added at the expense of the Society's president, Dr Tempest Anderson, in 1912. A large lecture theatre designed by Ridsdale Tate, it is attached to the museum and follows its height and style round the corner. But it is in fact wholly made of poured concrete, including the details – one of the earliest and most sophisticated uses of the modern medium.

81

ANN MIDDLETON'S HOSPITAL 1829
Skeldergate

The hospital for 20 widows of York freemen dates from the 17th century. This was a rebuilding, at the expense of the Corporation as one is reminded by the inscription, in 1829. It was modernised in 1939. It makes another quiet and restful urban space, set back from what is now a tatty service road that was once lined with handsome houses.

◀
80a

◀
80b

82
MOUNT PARADE c. 1830
The Mount

This is one of York's secrets. The Parade and the Terrace which joins it are hidden behind handsome Georgian houses on the Mount and on Holgate Road. There are some insertions of later doorways but most of them, and the general elegant style of the well-maintained houses, indicate their Regency date.

83
TOWER PLACE c. 1830
One of the most secret and secluded, and yet most central, of York's residential streets. The houses are set back from a paved passage with an inconspicuous entrance opposite Clifford's Tower. They are thus just inside the part of the medieval city wall which runs down from the castle to the river. The Regency terrace, with its shallow bays rising two storeys, makes a quietly elegant retreat in the heart of the city.

84
NEW WALK TERRACE c. 1830
The New Walk, stretching for half a mile from the confluence of the Ouse and the Foss along the river bank to the well-named Love Lane, was part of the Georgian transformation that made York a fashionable centre for a few years.

It was lined with trees and was started in 1733. The extension of the city thus begun was followed for the next 100 years by the building of terraces at right angles to the Walk. New Walk Terrace is the best; it has tall narrow houses with small rooms of taste and delicacy in the Regency style.

85
ST LEONARD'S PLACE   1831–5
The only place where a substantial section of the medieval wall has been removed: 350 ft of it between Bootham Bar and the Multangular Tower were cleared for the new crescent of 'elegant houses after a London style'. The houses are today occupied by offices of the Corporation. It is York's only but successful example of Regency urban design, later in date than its southern counterparts.

86
ST PETER'S SCHOOL   1837–8
Clifton
Architect: John Harper
In its earlier manifestations, St Peter's School dates back to the 7th century, but it was re-founded in 1557 under Mary Tudor. Shortly after transferring to a new building in the Minster precinct in 1833 (now the Minster Song School), it reached the nadir of its fortunes and was saved only by amalgamation with the Proprietary School at Clifton in 1844. It then moved, with its own name and a new reputation, to the buildings recently built for the Proprietary School Company. Cardboard Gothic in style, they give a suitable impression

of austere antiquity. Additional blocks were built in the 20th century, and from 1908 to 1919 the school took over several neighbouring old properties and thus preserved them.

87
OLD RAILWAY STATION   1838–41
Architect: G. T. Andrews
The first railway line to arrive in York was that of the York and North Midland Company in 1839. With other lines that were added in the next seven years it cut through the city wall and stopped at a terminus station. The Old Railway Station was designed by the York architect G. T. Andrews. Its long front was to Tanner Row, with rusticated stonework and rather Italianate arches above. Along the narrow front a hotel was added in 1853; it was superseded by the new hotel (103) and became offices.

88
CENTENARY METHODIST CHURCH
St Saviourgate   1839–40
Architect: James Simpson
Centenary Chapel was built, as its name suggests, to commemorate the centenary of Methodism. It was to be a 'cathedral' of Methodism and that is partly why it is so grand, with its giant Ionic portico, stone dressings and accommodation for 1,500 persons. It used to mark nobly the approach to the little street of St Saviourgate until a repellent modern building of indeterminate scale was inserted between them.

89
ST JOHN'S COLLEGE 1845
Lord Mayor's Walk
Architect: G. T. Andrews
Originally the York and Ripon Diocesan
Training College for schoolmasters, St John's
College grew into a substantial college of education, taking over in the 1960s the neighbouring buildings of Archbishop Holgate's Gram-
mar School, which moved to a collection of new
buildings on the outskirts of the city. Quiet and
dignified cardboard Gothic style with many
additional buildings at the back, the most
notable being the new chapel by George G.
Pace.

90
YORKSHIRE INSURANCE COMPANY
OFFICES 1847
St Helen's Square
Architect: G. T. Andrews
St Helen's Square was created out of the
churchyard of St Helen's Church, and later
widened to make it virtually the geographic
centre of the city. The Yorkshire's office is by
the architect who designed the railway station,
and is in fine ashlar, with sharp detail and
noble proportions – the image of a London
club.

91
ST GEORGE'S ROMAN CATHOLIC
CHURCH 1850
Peel Street
Architects: Joseph and Charles Hansom
The best of the Catholic churches. Its triple
gable at the west end is in the York tradition,
but equally in the handwriting of its architects,
who carried out many commissions for the
Catholic Church in the region. The interior
gives a pleasant impression of small scale
despite the size of the church, which was
needed to provide for the many Irish who had
arrived as immigrants in the Walmgate district
in the 1840s.

92
CAST IRON SHOPS *c.* 1850
Feasegate
Feasegate was widened in 1836, to coincide with
the opening of the new Parliament Street to
which it gave access. The cast-iron parts of the
buildings illustrated were made by Thomlinson

▶ 90

Walker, ironfounders of York, who were a firm of national stature; the railings of the National Gallery are by them. They went out of business in 1911. The decorated frame and panel construction made the building a pioneer in its time.

93
FRIARS TERRACE *c.* 1850
South Esplanade
The medieval Franciscan friary lay near here, between Castlegate and the Ouse. Not a trace of it remains; it was surrendered in 1538 and seems to have disappeared within 40 years. The original Friars Walk ran along the riverside downstream from the staith. Part of that ◀◀ 92 became the South Esplanade and set beside it is Friars Terrace – plain substantial Victorian townscape.

94
THE MOUNT SCHOOL   *c.* 1850
The Mount

Founded by the Quarterly Meetings as a school for the daughters of Friends, the school, a sister to Bootham, grew rapidly and took over much of the Mount. The house that forms the headquarters was bought in 1857. Its style is not as strange as a first impression suggests, for

it is painted in unusual tones to look like an outpost of the Empire.

95
YORK COUNTY HOSPITAL   1851
Monkgate

Architects: J. B. and W. Atkinson

The 18th-century hospital was in a square Georgian house on Monkgate. The present

building replaced it, but was set further back ◄◄ 96 to create a forecourt edged with ancillary buildings. The exterior is its best feature.

96
BANKS' MUSIC SHOP   *c.* 1860
Stonegate
The house which contains the shop is 18th-century, on older foundations. The shop front, brightly painted cast-iron, is Victorian, very fashionable.

97
WAREHOUSES   *c.* 1860
Queen's Staith
About the time of the building of Ouse Bridge, a new staith was constructed on the south bank of the river. This was Queen's Staith 1810–5; it was at first used for landing coal and was known as the Coal Staith. The warehouses that line it are becoming redundant and some have been removed, which is a pity; they add greatly to the character of the river, their bulk and regularity, with huge lettering and some remaining cranes in the foreground, recalling York's history as an inland port.

98
LENDAL BRIDGE   1861–2
Engineer: Thomas Page
At this point where the city walls stop on either bank of the Ouse there was for many centuries a ferry. The arrival of the railway made it necessary to have more than the one crossing, at Ouse Bridge, and the site of the ◄◄ 97 ferry was the obvious one. After 20 years of argument, a bridge by a designer with the ominous name of Dredge was started in 1860 but fell into the river in 1861; this one was by Thomas Page, the engineer of Westminster Bridge and a gifted designer of iron structures.

◄ 98

99
NEW RAILWAY STATION   1866–77
Architects: Thomas Prosser, Benjamin Burley and William Peachey

The New Station, which is the present one, was made necessary by growing traffic and the need for platforms on the through line. The famous curved train shed, with its prefabricated iron structure, heraldic details in the spandrels and subtle gradations of light as it filters through the glass section of the roof, was the work of three railway architects. The station became the largest in the country and the main platform the longest. The view from Platform 8 south into the shed is still the finest view in York; the station is York's propylaeum.

100
HEWORTH PARISH CHURCH   1867–9
East Parade
Architect: George Fowler Jones

The church of Holy Trinity is Early English in style (note the lancets and the plate tracery), and the church, both inside and out, is one of the most impressive Victorian churches in the city. The tower is in a most unusual position, presumably placed there to act as a dominant at the road junction.

101
THE YORKSHIRE CLUB   1868
Museum Street
Architect: C. J. Parnell

The Club was established in 1838 but moved into new premises at the end of the new Lendal Bridge. The Yorkshire Club was then considerably larger than it is today. The ungainly red brick buildings were designed in 1868 and are now a familiar landmark in the foreground of the most picturesque view of York, from the walls. It was the town centre for the country houses that surround York and Botterill's Horse Repositary (demolished) was just across the bridge. Lofty stair hall, excellent portraits of horses, especially in the Dining Room and the first floor Smoke Room (illustrated).

102
SKELDERGATE BRIDGE   1875–81
Engineers: Thomas and George Page

The river at the lower end of the city was crossed by a ferry when the engineer who had built the Lendal Bridge began his plan, identical in style and detailing, for Skeldergate Bridge. After his death his son completed the design, and the bridge was partly reconstructed in 1939. The stone arches over the land at the approaches to the bridge make ingenious walkways and attractive paths below. Above the bridge on the west bank, the illustration shows the mound of Baile Hill.

103
THE STATION HOTEL   1878–82
Architect: William Peachey

The Station Hotel was part of the design for the new station. Its front looks out on an incomparable view. Grand manner and boisterous if not pompous in its decor, its interior seems to invite both sedate and uproarious Victorian evenings.

104
CITY ART GALLERY   **1879**
Exhibition Square
Architect: Edward Taylor
The statue in the foreground, the centrepiece of
Exhibition Square, is of William Etty who was
a native of York and is well represented in the
collection. The gallery was the Yorkshire Fine
Art and Industrial Institution and was built
in 1879. The square was created out of a corner
of the Abbey grounds known as Bearpark's
Garden, but the Art Gallery as it later became
is too fragmentary and timid a piece of archi-
tecture to dominate it. Outstanding in the
collection is the Lycett Green bequest of
European masters.

105
LAW COURTS AND   **1890–2**
POLICE STATION
Clifford Street
Architect: Edmund Kirby
The police force was formed from a number of
disparate groups in 1836. The new law courts
and police station were won in an architectural
competition by a Liverpool architect, and
opened in 1892 in Clifford Street which, cut
through the old lanes on a curve in 1881 to join
Coney Street to the castle and courts, quickly
became a focus for civic buildings. More hideous
even than some of its contemporaries, it is
suitably awesome. The tower gives a view
across the city and the fire brigade is housed
beside the police, behind a depressingly vapid
modern façade.

106
LEETHAM'S MILL   *c.* 1895
Hungate
Architect: W. G. Penty
The river Foss originally widened out as it
curved round east of the city centre to form the
King's Fishponds. The city wall was interrupted
at this point. The ponds decayed and after silt-
ing up became known in the 18th century as
Foss Islands. In 1853 the Corporation bought

▶
106

▶
107a

he marshes from the Foss Navigation Company nd drained them. The Foss was realigned and Vormald's Cut made from the river into the dustrial area. Leetham's roller flour mill was uilt on its bank; it became a major industry nd remains the most impressive 19th-century dustrial building in York.

107
SCARCROFT ROAD SCHOOL and 1896
POPPLETON ROAD SCHOOL 1904
Architect: W. H. Brierley
Two of the three schools in York by Brierley. They are planned in accordance with the school regulations of the end of the 19th century and

Art Nouveau. The schools are of brick and are devoid of any but original detail, their composition works by mass and plane.

108
HUNT'S BREWERY 189
Aldwark

Immediately inside the city walls are area which developed with industry, warehousing and industrial housing in the 19th century. The Ebor Brewery, with its brick walls, pantiled roofs and louvred caps, is a good example of the functional tradition.

109
YORK DISPENSARY 189
Duncombe Place
Architect: Edmund Kirby

Of shining and apparently imperishable re brick, the Dispensary was opened in Duncombe Place in 1899. The architect used speciall moulded bricks as well as stone and terracott to achieve the decorative richness of the façade Often ignored behind the trees, it forms with its neighbours an admirable stretch of urba architecture. The Dispensary was founded i 1788 and wound up in 1949 after the intro duction of the National Health Service, to b used subsequently as offices.

are exercises in functional planning that fore-shadowed many of the design features of modern architecture. In style they are influenced by pioneers such as Charles Rennie Mackintosh and by the decorative work associated with the Arts and Crafts movement; there are overtones of the Pre-Raphaelites and

110
THE OLD STAR Interior lat
Stonegate 19th Centur

York is littered with public houses. The architectural climax must have occurred short before 1900, when the interiors of some of th most distinctively local took on their presen

hape. The Star in Stonegate has, as well as porting prints, timber-lined walls and partitions making small spaces and comfortable orners in the smoke room and snug.

boarded ceilings have been retained, pictures, trim and furnishings of the period brought in, and the result could not be bettered by the Castle Museum. Sloping floors and a series of varied and glittering spaces.

11

THE BAY HORSE Interior late
Blossom Street **19th Century and 1969**
Architects for restoration: John Smith's Architects Department

Restored by the brewery's own architects in he late 1960s, the Bay Horse had not been altered since the 1890s. The tobacco-stained

112

THE BLUEBELL Late 19th
Fossgate **Century**

Despite a glazed brick façade and a nondescript front bar, the Bluebell has the best inner bar in the city. Very small, very genuine, lovingly maintained by the landlady, as by her mother before her.

but its interiors are startling. The only elaborat
specimen of Art Nouveau decor in York, it i
also one of the most complete and superior i
the country. Its author was George Walton, th
Glasgow designer and contemporary o
Mackintosh, who moved to England and ha
for a time a shop in Stonegate. Note th
attenuated woodwork, the beaten coppe
fitments and the frescos made with dyes an
beset with glass jewels.

114
BARCLAYS BANK   190
Parliament Street
Architect: Edmund Kirby
At the corner of Parliament Street and Higl
Ousegate, Barclays Bank was thought for man
years to be in the worst possible taste; but tast
has changed and now it is a highly regarded and
distinctive landmark. Like other buildings o
its date it is made of hard shiny brick-lik
materials which seem immune to weathering
or to any of the other forces of erosion whicl
soften the lines of mercantile palaces and rende
them gentler to see. The boarded windows ar
the sign, not of student protest about the bank'
foreign investments, but of internal alteration
designed to modernise the bank while retainin
its memorable exterior.

113
ELM BANK HOTEL   Interior 1900
The Mount
*Architect: W. G. Penty: interior designed by
George Walton*
The Elm Bank Hotel is a rather forbidding
19th-century structure recast by W. G. Penty,

115
NEW EARSWICK GARDEN VILLAGE
                                 1901 and late
Architects: Raymond Unwin and Barry Parker
This garden village was the brainchild o
Joseph Rowntree, the owner of the Coco

Works and a leading figure in the movement for improved housing and community planning at the turn of the century. He acquired land 3 miles north of the Works and built a model village of 500 homes, surrounded by a green belt to separate it from the city. It has a village council, two schools, a Folk Hall (135) and is run by a Village Trust, which ensures that the community does not have a majority of Cocoa Works employees. Houses, orientated to the sunlight, surrounded by gardens and built of traditional materials, are grouped around cul-de-sacs in a layout linked by a main perimeter road and crossed by a footpath system.

116

SOUTH AFRICAN WAR MEMORIAL

Duncombe Place   **1905**
Architect: G. F. Bodley

The Boer War attracted many volunteers from Yorkshire and the memorial commemorates 1,320 of them who lost their lives. A thickly carved octagonal column sitting on steps and with a lantern on top, it is well placed in the green space at the end of Duncombe Place but fails to attract much attention. It is after all somewhat overshadowed by the Minster. None the less some lightning in 1961 managed to miss the Minster and hit the memorial instead.

117
BISHOPSBARNS   **1905**
5 St George's Place
Architect: W. H. Brierley

Walter Brierley's firm was the descendant of those of Carr of York and the Atkinsons, father and son. His practice was extensive and included work on large private houses, public buildings and schools. He was the most original architect York nurtured before the present day. His own house confirms his place in the English tradition, which from 1890 to World War I and for a few years after gave 'Das englische Haus' international fame; the English-

man's house was humane, personal, homely, informal, traditional in materials, excellently constructed and well serviced.

118
RAILWAY OFFICES   **1906**
Architects: Horace Field and William Bell

With offices in the Old Station, the new offices were built facing them and the height of buildings in York began to rise. They are in a version of Norman Shaw's Queen Anne style, with well proportioned fenestration and heroic rows of dormers.

119
MACDONALD'S 1911 and later
Fossgate

Films, or animated pictures, began to be shown in the early years of the 20th century, but this was the first building in York to be specifically designed as a cinema. It was called the Electric and beckoned the viewer in through a huge arch with overtones of the 'naughty nineties', and carved swags of fruit and hideous masks. Though renamed the Scala in 1951, it did not revive and was sold for use as shops in 1957.

120
JOSEPH TERRY AND SONS 1926
Bishopthorpe Works

The oldest confectionery business in York, Terry's was founded in the centre of the city in the 18th century, expanded rapidly in the middle of the 19th century so that the company moved to new premises outside the city wall, and in 1926 built the modern factory illustrated. Handsomely designed in a debased neoclassical style, it overlooks the Knavesmire and Racecourse, its tower a landmark.

the Museum Gardens and the Multangular
Tower.

121
THE CITY LIBRARY   1927, 1938
Museum Street
Architects: Brierley, Rutherford and Syme
The Public Library was founded in 1893. In
1924 it received a grant from the Carnegie
Trustees and the new building was built on the
site of the medieval St Leonard's Hospital. It
was extended in 1938. In civic classical style,
the side elevation is the best; it looks out on to

122
THE JOHN BURRILL ALMSHOUSES
Clifton   1931
Seven single-storey houses on three sides of a
green. Pleasant unassertive dwellings, they
capture the essence of the English contribution
to domestic architecture in the early years of

the century, a fusion of anonymous-looking dwellings with homely landscape.

123
GALTRES GROVE 1936
Clifton
Architect: Barry Parker
Part of the Clifton Lodge estate developed by the Rowntree trusts after World War I. The estate was developed between 1926 and 1936. In reality it was completed even later, if at all, for it is essentially an environment of houses, gardens and organic landscape. Some of the houses have Parker's innovation – 'through'

living rooms to give flexibility of orientation – which are now a commonplace, and rational plans that anticipated much post-1945 housing.

124
THE ODEON 1937
Blossom Street
Architect: Harry W. Weedon
The most handsome of the York cinemas. Local opinion persuaded the owners to build the façade in facing brick and thus lend some dignity and local character to the usual meretricious cinema style. With the closing of many cinemas, including a number of those built in

the 1930s, the Odeon will shortly be an historic building, a valued relic of the era of exaggerated verticals and softened cubism.

125
COLLEGE OF FURTHER EDUCATION
Dringhouses   **1960–8**
Architects: City Architect's Department
In the 1960s further education was regrouped and a comprehensive scheme of new buildings was developed at the edge of the city. The development is in four stages and includes blocks for engineering, building, administration and commerce, the last of which was completed in 1968.

125 ▶

126
ASKHAM BRYAN COLLEGE OF AGRICULTURE   **1961 and later**
Architects: Brierley, Leckenby and Keighley
Outside the city boundary looking across the road to Tadcaster, the College of Agriculture has been continuously developed since 1961. The layout and buildings include hostels, workshops, teaching buildings, halls, houses, a science block, and the Assembly Hall which is illustrated and dates from 1963.

127
UNIVERSITY OF YORK   **1962 and later**
Heslington
Architects: Robert Matthew, Johnson-Marshall and Partners
The city of York made petitions to the government for the establishment of a university in 1641 and 1648; the request was finally granted in 1962. From a small number of old buildings in the city centre it grew steadily and with an unusual speed of building. The main part of the new university was planned as a collegiate community on a site of 185 acres that formed the grounds of the 16th- and 19th-century Heslington Hall. In so far as there is one, its centre is a plastic-bottomed lake; colleges, science laboratories and central function buildings form a continuous development that starts with the Hall and reaches to the boundaries of the city. The colleges are built in CLASP, a system of prefabricated components with a light steel frame and cladding panels, developed for schools; the cladding panels of concrete were designed for university conditions and have since become a standard component for the system. It gives the colleges a repetitive appearance in detail but not at all in plan and mass; they are varied and their interiors carefully distinguished from each other. Some central buildings are not in the system, notably the Central Hall, the Library, one of the Laboratories and the water tower that looms

126 ▶

over the chemistry laboratories – an unforeseen ◀◀
requirement that was transformed into a
triumphant improvisation. But what makes the
University as a whole an exceptional landmark
in modern architectural design is not any of
its individual buildings but its quality as an
environment. With the exception of the flam-
boyant Central Hall it consists of grey buildings
set anonymously in a richly planted landscape:
exactly and uniquely what the architects and
client intended in the first place.

128
HALF MOON COURT   1963
Castle Museum
Architect: R. Patterson
The presentation of bygones by putting them in
their context in rebuilt old houses and shops
was begun in 1938 when the collection of Dr
Kirk of Pickering was taken over by the
Corporation. The first – and most elaborate –
street is in the Female Prison (68). But in 1952
the Debtors' Prison (52) was adapted as an
extension to the museum and in 1963 (with
considerable celebration) another street was
opened. It too uses demolished buildings and
contains exciting displays of obsolete electrical
goods and a public house which had disappeared

from the city. Half Moon Court gives an impression of a York street of the period that ended with World War I.

129
YORK CREMATORIUM 1963
Bishopthorpe
Architects: City Architect's Department
Since the building of Asplund's crematorium in Stockholm, crematoria have seemed peculiarly tractable to modern architecture. Their functional programme lends itself to coherent massing and inspires a simple but evocative

design. Beautifully sited, the crematorium is one of the most successful new buildings in or near the city.

130
CHURCH OF THE HOLY REDEEMER
Boroughbridge Road 1964
Architect: George G. Pace
An impeccable example of liturgical church design by York's eminent ecclesiastical architect, George G. Pace. The medieval church of St Bishophill Senior was taken down in the 1960s. Its columns and some of its stonework were carried to Boroughbridge Road and incorporated into an otherwise uncompromisingly contemporary church distinguished by many of Mr Pace's most personal design features – a confirmation that if both kinds of architecture are strong and definite enough they can live together happily.

131
YORK RACECOURSE 1965
Knavesmire
Architects: Rainger, Roger and Smithson
A study in change of scale. Racing is a traditional activity of York, and the Knavesmire has been used for it since 1731. The stands were then designed by Carr of York but none of his work remains. They were replaced by the decorative 1834 stand which looked gay and lavish until the new, inelegant but efficient one was built alongside, thus notably raising the standards of the course, and dwarfing its predecessor.

132
LINDSEY AVENUE HOUSING 1965-70
Architects: City Architect's Department
An attractive project of local authority housing by the City Architect's department. It is a mixed development of terraced houses, old people's dwellings and 4-storey maisonettes,

▶
128

▶
129

grouped effectively on the low hilltop above Acomb, creating small sheltered spaces and a humane environment.

133
BOOTHAM SCHOOL ASSEMBLY
HALL   1966
Architects: Trevor Dannatt and Partners
An outstanding modern building in York that won the RIBA award for Yorkshire. It seats

nearly 500 and is used for assembly, worship, lectures, concerts, theatre and opera; the design of multi-purpose halls like that is not easy. It is free standing, at the back of the Georgian school building, so as not to obstruct a view of the Minster. But its quality lies in its sculptural individuality, created by the clearcut forms of shutter-marked concrete, the open corners, the sheets of glass sliding into the concrete and the boldly modelled copper-covered roof. The

interior is as strong and evocative as the exterior promises. The structure was designed by Ove Arup and partners.

134
UNIVERSITY HOUSING AT BLEACHFIELD 1967
Heslington
Architects: York University Design Unit
This was the first work of the York University Design Unit founded as the nucleus of a teaching office for the proposed school of architecture in the University. Twenty-two houses in brick with timber upper floors, they are

designed so as to allow varied groupings of rooms between dwellings. They received a Ministry of Housing Award in 1968.

135
FOLK HALL and SWIMMING POOL 1968
New Earswick
Architects: Robert Matthew, Johnson-Marshall and Partners
The social centre of the garden village of New Earswick required alterations to bring it more in line with modern demands. In keeping with the ideology of Joseph Rowntree who had

visualised the whole settlement as an example of community planning, the alterations and additions to Unwin's hall became more than an architectural project. The trustees of the Village Trust, the Village Council and residents combined in the briefing of the architects; the hall was redesigned making sitting spaces, coffee bars, a nursery and welfare clinic; and a terrace looks towards the new swimming pool whose modern lines and traditional materials make it an entirely appropriate addition to the village.

136
N.E.E.B. CONTROL CENTRE 1968
Hungate
Architects: L. J. Couves and Partners
Although within the city centre, this develop-

ment is not on any main route and escapes observation – a pity, because, apart from detailed drawbacks, it is a good example of clean massing, unobtrusive design and the use of modern materials for a modern function within an old city.

137
PATCH HOUSE 1968
Heslington
Architects: Booton and Farmer
A neat imaginative single-storey open planned new house for a University teacher. It is in the village of Heslington and lurks behind an old brick wall which is cleverly overlapped by the deep edge of its flat roof, that gives promise of something interesting behind. The house thus

sits undisturbed among Georgian neighbours, and would be just as effective if it were more open to view.

138
THE TAVERN IN THE TOWN 1968
Ouse Bridge
Architects: Chef and Brewer Ltd.'s Architects' Department
The former brewery on the edge of the Ouse close to Ouse Bridge is reached by a footway along a modern building or from a court on the other side. Thus it seems almost, but not quite, natural to stroll into a pub of many different periods littered with booths and barnacles and nets and buoys. The illustrations show the Dickens Grill and the Cellar Bar. It is a cleverly contrived and wholly artificial environment that appeals to all one's worst architectural instincts.

139

THE VIKING HOTEL   **1968**

North Street

Architects: Fitzroy Robinson and Partners

An 8-storey slab block on a podium, the Viking Hotel has the characteristic form of many modern buildings. It also has an incomparable position on the bank of the river Ouse, opposite the Guildhall and beside a small public garden. Acceptable in itself, it may be questioned whether this kind of building, with its height, mass and form, makes any contribution to York's architecture, or is essentially in conflict with the underlying grain of the city.

140
WHITE ROSE HOUSING
SOCIETY 1968–9
Heslington Road
Architect: James Williams
Near the University site at Heslington but in
no way dominated by it visually or socially, the
development includes 27 houses and flats and
two attractive studios, grouped around a
common space well landscaped and reflecting
the neat and unaggressive character of the
houses themselves. The scheme set a standard
for co-operative housing.

141
CHALFONTS 1969
Tadcaster Road
Architects: Shepherd Design Group
Speculative housing by a builder at its best.
There are 12 houses around a green that pro-

vides social and play space, and the whole group
is set conveniently away from the main road
over the slope of a hill. The project received a
housing award from the Ministry of Housing
and Local Government in 1969.

142
EDMUND WILSON SWIMMING
BATH 1969
Acomb
Architects: City Architect's Department
A popular and much-needed amenity in the
major residential district of Acomb, a suburb
incorporated into York and one in which many
more people live today than did in the whole
of the medieval city. There are two pools,
offices and a coffee bar; the straightforward
manner of the building sets a new standard for
the depressingly uninspired housing that sur-
rounds it.

143
HUDSON HOUSE 1969
Toft Green
Architects: British Rail, Regional Architects'
Department

A wholly straightforward and well designed
modern building of glass and prefabricated
concrete wall units, the offices for British Rail
Eastern Region are unpretentious and satisfying. They are beside the medieval wall, which
dictates their height and suggests the kind
of aggregate in the concrete. Emphasis is given
to the elevations by the projection of the floors
created by the splays below and above the
windows.

144
HOLMFIELD HOUSING SOCIETY
Heslington 1969–71
Architects: York University Design Unit

Behind the village street and forming part of
the proposed village development, the first
phase of the Society's project includes 33
houses and flats, faced with selected common
bricks, boldly massed and in an uncompromising way recapturing much of the character
of the older buildings in the village. The
scheme includes 94 houses and flats, occupied
mainly by members of the University.

INDEX